SOFT CORALS

AND RELATED MINI-REEF ANIMALS

Jim Fatherree

As interest in the aquarium hobby continues to grow every year, more and more people are becoming involved in the husbandry of live corals and other marine invertebrates. Keeping these animals alive and well in reef aquariums can be a very interesting and rewarding pastime if done properly, but this requires that hobbyists teach themselves all aspects of the hobby from filtration techniques to lighting systems to the individual living requirements of each and every type of organism they want to keep. Failure to do so most commonly results in complete loss and leads to nothing but frustration for the not-yet-educated aquarist. So although a major aim of this publication will be to provide readers with a basic background in the biology and natural history of the various animals it covers and to color that information in light of some of the purely aquaristic concerns involved with the needs of soft corals and their relatives, how to choose and use marine aquarium equipment will not be a major part of this book. Certainly attention will be paid to such vital considerations as nitrite and nitrate buildup, pH and temperature, but there will be no in-depth discussions of currently available filtration strategies and water treatment systems and things of that nature—those are for the many good specialized marine aquarium books already on the market. Here we'll talk mostly about and show the animals known as soft corals in the aquarium hobby from the standpoint of showing where they fit taxonomically and how they differ from one another, coupled with discussions of their particular requirements as aquarium dwellers: what they have to have and what has to be avoided.

Distributed in the UNITED STATES to the Pet Trade by T.F.H. Publications, Inc., One T.F.H. Plaza, Neptune City, NJ 07753; on the Internet at www.tfh.com; in CANADA Rolf C. Hagen Inc., 3225 Sartelon St. Laurent-Montreal Quebec H4R 1E8; Pet Trade by H & L Pet Supplies Inc., 27 Kingston Crescent, Kitchener, Ontario N2B 2T6; in ENGLAND by T.F.H. Publications, PO Box 15, Waterlooville PO7 6BQ; in AUSTRALIA AND THE SOUTH PACIFIC by T.F.H. (Australia), Pty. Ltd., Box 149, Brookvale 2100 N.S.W., Australia; in NEW ZEALAND by Brooklands Aquarium Ltd. 5 McGiven Drive, New Plymouth, RD1 New Zealand; in SOUTH AFRICA, Rolf C. Hagen S.A. (PTY.) LTD. P.O. Box 201199, Durban North 4016, South Africa; in Japan by T.F.H. Publications, Japan—Jiro Tsuda, 10-12-3 Ohjidai, Sakura, Chiba 285, Japan. Published by T.F.H. Publications, Inc.
MANUFACTURED IN THE
UNITED STATES OF AMERICA
BY T.F.H. PUBLICATIONS, INC.

CONTENTS

Photos by the author except as specifically noted otherwise.

INTRODUCTION

Two of the most prominent and popular groups of marine invertebrates suitable for life in the reef aquarium are the soft corals and the sea anemones. Many of the soft corals, as they are commonly called by hobbyists, are actually not corals at all but are just relatives of the true corals and are only called so for convenience. They include a wide range of organisms, including the leather corals, the star polyps, the sea whips and sea fans, the colonial anemones and the mushroom anemones. Those animals, along with the true sea anemones, all belong to a very large common group within the class Anthozoa in the phylum Cnidaria (formerly known as the phylum Coelenterata). There are many other animals in the phylum Cnidaria— jellyfishes, hydras, the Portuguese man o'war and the sea wasps are just a few of the animals contained in other classes within the phylum—but we're not greatly involved with them in this book.

Each of these anthozoan groups and the wide variety of species that each is composed of occupy their own niches in the reef environment. Each has its own particular water current preferences. Each thrives in a particular range of lighting intensity. And each acts as aggressor to—or victim of—other cnidarians nearby. For this reason, this book can be a valuable resource for hobbyists hungry for answers and ready to build their own personal reef ecosystems.

This book will cover the basic aspects of cnidarian anatomy and cnidarian environmental requirements, including water quality and lighting needs, and how to avoid specimens that are in poor condition or otherwise unsuitable when making purchases. Specific information concerning such topics as identification, reproduction, nutritional requirements and general hardiness of each of the aforementioned types of soft corals and sea anemones is also provided. You can't be expected to absorb all of the information at one reading, so keep this publication around and remember to refer back to it as needed in the future.

A view into a 60-gallon reef tank dominated by several types of soft corals, including a toadstool leather coral, a finger leather coral, a lettuce coral and a sea fan.

A 75-gallon reef aquarium featuring different soft corals.

Hard and soft corals co-exist in this 20-gallon reef tank.

Above: A toadstool leather coral (upper left), some sun polyps (slightly below and to right of leather coral) and mushroom anemones all living in almost direct contact with one another. Proximity to other soft corals is an important factor in determining which soft corals can be accommodated in a reef tank.

Left: This 200-gallon reef tank contains more than a dozen taxonomic groups of soft corals and anemones.

ALL ABOUT CNIDARIANS

Corals, sea anemones, jellyfish and other related animals all belong to the biological group known as the phylum Cnidaria (pronounced ny-*dar*-ree-ah; the "C" is silent). This biological group of animals first appeared on Earth in ancient seas during the development of multicellular organisms well over a half billion years ago and has given rise to almost countless species of jellyfish, hard and soft corals, sea anemones and other related organisms.

While thousands of these species have been thoroughly studied by scientists, the early history of this phylum is at best sketchy. That is because scientists must depend upon fossil evidence found in rocks to build a detailed history, but unfortunately many of the members of the phylum did not possess hard skeletons that could be preserved as fossils. When an early cnidarian died there was nothing durable to be preserved, and the oldest cnidarian fossils that scientists have discovered are simply imprints of jellyfish-like organisms that were buried in fine sediments before they decomposed. It is clear that such preservation would be a rare occurrence, and these types of fossils are few and far between. Still it is

A specimen of *Rhodactis,* one of the genera of corallimorph cnidarians. This large mushroom anemone is a good example of a cnidarian that lives as a solitary animal. Notice the centrally situated bump, which is the opening to its mouth.

This cluster of sun polyps may look like a group of individual polyps at first glance, but on closer inspection it can be seen that they're all joined by a common fleshy base and are therefore colonial cnidarians.

thought that all of the first cnidarians were free-living organisms and that over millions of years some of them eventually took on a life attached to the bottom. Through time many of these sedentary groups also began to form complex colonies composed of hundreds or thousands of intimately connected organisms. From these primordial groups arose all of the incredible varieties of solitary and colonial cnidarians that we strive to keep alive and well in our reef aquariums today.

THE BASIC ANATOMY OF CNIDARIANS

Cnidarians are biologically among the simplest of the multi-cellular animals, and while their overall external appearance may vary greatly, they are all very similar in a number of ways. First, all cnidarians have the same basic body construction at the tissue level of organization. All have a body wall composed of an outer and inner layer. The outermost layer is called the ectodermis, or ectoderm, and is comparable to the animal's "skin"; the innermost layer is called the endodermis, endoderm or gastrodermis. Between these two layers is a clear jelly-like material called the mesoglea.

Typical cnidarians have a prominent mouth that opens into a large single body cavity. Cnidarians have no true digestive system or tract, but this cavity acts as the organism's stomach and is called the enteron, or gastrovascular cavity. In this area food is held and digested through the use of various enzymes. Nutrients are then absorbed by the cells of the gastrodermis and are spread throughout the organism's body by cell-to-cell transfer. Cnidarians have no excretory system either, and after food has undergone digestion wastes are simply ejected back through the mouth or are secreted through the body and out to the environment through the cells of the ectoderm.

The mouth is typically surrounded by a ring of tentacles of varying size. The primary function of these tentacles is to help the organism capture and ingest food. To aid in this task any ten-

Sarcophyton, one of the leather corals, commonly thus called because of the leathery feeling of the base from which the individual polyps emerge.

tacles present are usually covered by thousands of specialized cells called cnidocytes, which are unique to cnidarians. In fact, the name of these cells is the basis for the name of the phylum. Cnidocytes come in three basic forms: glutinant, volvant and penetrant. The volvant and glutinant types are used to entangle prey and may also be used to help the organism stick to a surface. Penetrant cnidocytes are commonly called nematocysts and are similar to tiny poisonous harpoons. These cells can explode outward, shooting a tiny toxic barb into an attacker as a defensive measure or into a prey organism during the capture of food. These tiny poison harpoons are well known in cnidarians such as stinging jellyfish and the fire corals. However, very few if any cnidarians available to hobbyists carry such a powerful punch. Most cannot even give you a sting that is feelable through the thick skin on your hands.

Cnidarians also lack respiratory systems, and although they live their lives submerged within the sea, they have no gills. They acquire much-needed oxygen by simple

Above: Members of the order Alcyonacea, the leather corals, vary greatly in form and color. The leather coral shown in the center of the photo above is a *Sarcophyton* species; the leather coral shown at right is a *Sinularia* species.

osmosis, absorbing it directly from the seawater that constantly bathes them over their entire body surface. Cnidarians also have no pulmonary system. There is no beating heart, no veins, no arteries. No blood. As mentioned, nutrients are simply passed from cell to cell throughout the body. They don't have a central nervous system either. No brain. All that is present in most is a simple "nerve net" made of a few elongated neurons. It's hard to understand how such simple animals have been so successful, but they have!

Different cnidarians can be found as individual animals or as members of complex colonies. Each animal, whether an individual or a part of a colony, is called a polyp, and each polyp has a mouth, a gastrovascular cavity and other cnidarian anatomical features. Often in the colonial cnidarians each polyp can be so well integrated with the

Organ-pipe coral, often confused with the hard corals (order Scleractinia) because of the red tubes it produces, is actually a member of the order Stolonifera, the star polyps

In the foreground is a typical gorgonian, one of the sea whips of the order Gorgonacea.

surrounding polyps that it is practically impossible to tell where one polyp stops and another starts, because they actually share a common ectodermis and mesoglea. In such cases the tissues of these cnidarians are so intimately connected that the colony lives as if it were one organism, sharing the food and nutrients taken in and produced by each individual polyp.

CNIDARIAN FEEDING AND ALGAL SYMBIOSIS

Many cnidarians are carnivorous, eating anything from the smallest plankton to relatively large fish. Cnidarians that have rela-

Photos above and below show groups of mushroom anemones of the genus *Actinodiscus* . The corallimorphs do not rely on zooxanthellae for the provision of nutrients; they are able to catch their food.

Star polyps of the genus *Clavularia*. Unlike the organ-pipe corals (genus *Tubipora*) of the order Stolonifera, these stoloniferans don't build red tubes.

tively large tentacles often grab onto and eat anything meaty that they can get a grip on, while those that do not have large tentacles, or have no obvious tentacles at all, cover themselves with a thin layer of mucus; the layer of mucus is used to collect bacteria and plankton as if it were fly-paper. This mucous sheet is then "reeled in" to the mouth and moved to the gastrovascular cavity, where the food particles are digested. Some cnidarians use both of these methods of feeding.

Many cnidarians, especially hard corals, also receive large amounts of nutrients from single-celled algae-like organisms that live in their tissues. These tiny organisms are called zooxanthellae and are a type of dinoflagellate belonging to the genus *Symbiodinium*. The relationship between the cnidarian host and its zooxanthellae is called a symbiosis. In this case both the cnidarian and the algae receive benefits from each other. The zooxanthellae provide the animal's cells with a constant internal source of oxygen, carbohydrates and a variety of other vital nutrients produced during photosynthesis. The zooxanthellae also take up some of the waste carbon dioxide produced by the cnidarian's cells during metabolism. This greatly enhances the ability for gas exchange in an organism that lacks a respiratory system. In return, the animal provides the algae with a place to call home as well as a source of carbon dioxide, phosphate and other required nutrients.

This symbiotic relationship is the reason that every time you've seen a picture of a thriving coral reef it has been in shallow, clear, warm water. The zooxanthellae will survive only if water temperatures stay in the mid sixties to the upper eighties (Fahrenheit), and they need intense sunlight in order to carry out normal photosynthetic processes while deep inside the cnidarian's tissues. For this reason symbiotic cnidarians are almost always found at depths of less than 150 feet; it is very rare to find them in waters deeper than 300 feet.

Some of the aggressive "sweeper" tentacles of a *Plerogyra* species, one of the hard corals. The soft corals, like the hard corals, differ in their tendencies to be aggressive against other cnidarians and in the amount of damage they can do.

THE WEAPONS OF CNIDARIANS

Cnidarians that live their lives attached to the seafloor in a reef environment must compete for growing space on the reef while simultaneously attempting to protect themselves from predation by a variety of other organisms. The basic weapons that some cnidarians employ to ensure their own survival are called acontia. The acontia are thin extrudable digestive filaments that are normally kept inside the gastrovascular cavity. If something irritating or threatening comes into contact with particular cnidarians, these filaments are extruded through the mouth and quickly begin secreting diges-

tive substances directly onto whatever they touch. This action can cause serious tissue damage to the victim and can be very effective for close-quarters fighting amongst neighbors.

As discussed, many cnidarians also have tentacles surrounding their mouths or the perimeter of the body that can deliver a nasty sting using nematocysts. Nematocysts are very sensitive to physical contact with an object but also usually require chemical stimulation by an organic substance in order to "fire." This keeps them from constantly firing every time they come into contact with non-threatening objects and non-prey items such as rocks.

Lastly, many cnidarians also have the ability to produce waterborne toxins. These toxic substances, called terpenoids, are released to spread through the surrounding water, where they irritate or poison other cnidarians that are too close. This type of defense (or offense) is very effective and can commonly lead to the demise of a variety of other cnidarians, especially in the closed environment of aquariums.

CNIDARIAN REPRODUCTION

Cnidarians reproduce sexually and asexually a number of different ways. Typically the most common method among cnidarians is asexual reproduction, in which neither sperm nor eggs are produced. Many cnidarians can produce "buds" that grow from the parent and eventually get big enough to tear away and form a new individual or colony. Other cnidarians reproduce asexually, through fragmentation. This can be a product of the organism's splitting itself into two or more pieces that all grow into adults, or of the organism's being torn into pieces by predators or storms. While these methods are simple and require little or no energy, they also form only genetic clones of the parents, which gives rise to the problems of insufficient genetic mixing within the species.

Many cnidarians are hermaphroditic spawners, producing both eggs and sperm that are ejected directly into surrounding waters, where they will with luck run into each other and the eggs and sperm of their neighbors to produce new offspring. This method of sexual reproduction allows the coral's offspring to spread over a wide geographic range by drifting in currents. It also allows for a certain degree of genetic variability through mixing, which is required in order to adapt to any environmental changes through natural selection. Still other cnidarians are "brooders" that undergo internal self-fertilization. After self-fertilization the parent holds the juvenile offspring internally for some period of time and then releases them into the surrounding waters. This method of reproduction provides the offspring with a "head start."

Both of these types of sexual reproduction require the organism to use a considerable amount of energy to produce sperm and eggs; they therefore are not always the best methods of reproduction either. That is why it is common for cnidarians to use both sexual and asexual methods of reproduction,

The photos above and below illustrate reproduction of a mushroom anemone by auto-fragmentation. The upper photo shows the expanded healthy "parent" organism; the lower photo show the parent corallimorph shriveled and in the process of division.

depending on environmental conditions such as food supply.

THE TAXONOMY OF CNIDARIANS

The phylum Cnidaria comprises more than 9000 species of animals that can be found in an incredible range of shapes, sizes and colors. Also, while reef cnidarians are restricted to warm shallow water, others can be found in almost all marine settings; a few have even adapted to life in fresh waters.

The accompanying text presents the general classification of the modern cnidarians, broken down class by class within the phylum. Cnidarian taxonomy is based on several characters, from overall structure to different life cycles to the number of tentacles each polyp of a particular group has, and in some instances species are so hard to tell apart that a microscope is required to look for the tiny differences in their structures. It can be quite difficult and for the most part should be left to the experts. There have also been nomenclatural changes over the years, resulting from the restructuring of various groups. So it is common to see different names for the same taxonomic group in aquarium literature. The entire phylum Cnidaria, for instance, was called the phylum Coelenterata not too long ago, and of course individuals within the class were called coelenterates instead of cnidarians. The phylum contains four different classes: Hydrozoa (which comprises seven orders and includes such dangerous animals as the Portuguese man o' war and the fire corals); Scyphozoa (the jellyfishes); Cubozoa (the sea wasps); and the Anthozoa, wherein we find the animals that are the subject of this publication.

The soft-bodied cnidarians that are commonly found in reef aquariums and are our primary subjects of discussion all belong to the class Anthozoa (the most "important" members of which are the hard corals and the anemones), but they are spread over two different subclasses within the Anthozoa. The subclass Alcyonaria (also known as Octocorallia) contains the leather corals (order Alcyonacea), the gorgonians, sea fans and sea whips (order Gorgonacea) and the organ pipe corals and star polyps (order Stolonifera). The subclass Zoantharia contains the colonial anemones (order Zoanthidea), the mushroom anemones (order Corallimorpharia) and the true anemones (order Actiniaria). Both subclasses also contain other orders, but we're not concerned with those orders here, since we're dealing only with the cnidarians generally regarded as "soft corals." (The "hard corals, " incidentally, are within the order Scleractinia, subclass Zoantharia.) Each of the pertinent groups will be discussed in detail in the sections that follow.

An anemone of the order Actiniaria, commonly designated as the true anemones, with a guest anemonefish (*Amphiprion*). A gorgonian can be seen in the background.

RE-CREATING THE REEF ENVIRONMENT

In an effort to keep soft corals and anemones healthy in the closed environment of an aquarium hobbyists must pay close attention to the various aspects of water quality and lighting. You must attempt to recreate the animals' natural environment on the reef as well as possible. It should be noted that while much of the information that follows is pertinent to all marine aquariums, much is specifically aimed at the care of these organisms and is therefore very important to the reef hobbyist.

TEMPERATURE

Air temperatures in the tropics can vary by tens of degrees from day to night and day to day. However, the temperature of sea water around most coral reefs fluctuates only ten to fifteen degrees Fahrenheit over the period of an entire year, changing only slightly from week to week or month to month. Water temperatures commonly are even more stable than that in many areas of the world. Water temperature control is therefore an important part of keeping any reef aquarium. The water temperature of your

One of the characteristics of the coral reefs is the stability of the conditions under which they've grown; temperatures, salinity factors and lighting duration and quality remain basically the same throughout the year. This photo is of a reef off North Palawan in the Philippines. Photo by Guy van den Bossche.

The reefs harbor a great variety of life forms, from invertebrates such as the corals and sponges and crustaceans and echinoderms that live on and around them right up through the vertebrates—primarily the fishes—that also depend on them for shelter and food. Photo by Cathy Church.

peratures fluctuate several degrees around reefs, as mentioned, the changes are usually very slow. The temperature may vary much less than one degree per month as seasons change. Therefore the water temperature of your aquarium should not only be kept within this range but also should be kept as stable as possible. Constant swings in temperature can stress aquarium inhabitants and should be kept at a minimum.

A good-quality submersible heater with an adjustable thermostat will do a good job of keeping water temperatures within the correct range and stable during cold winter months if required, but in most cases the aquarium's water will need to be cooled down rather than heated up. This results from the excessive heat produced by most high-output lighting systems used for keeping reef aquariums. If this is the case, fans may be used to cool light bulbs and can also be positioned to blow across the surface of the aquarium water, promoting the rapid evaporation and consequent cooling of the water.

This usually is sufficient, but in extreme cases it may be necessary to buy a water chiller made specifically for the job. These are basically small refrigerators made so that water can be pumped into them, cooled down and pumped back into the aquarium. Unfortunately, chillers are usually rather expensive.

SPECIFIC GRAVITY

Specific gravity is a common way to measure the "saltiness" of water by com-

reef aquarium should always stay within the same temperature range that corals and anemones experience in their natural environment. Tied in with temperature is oxygen content, because the amount of oxygen dissolved in sea water is strongly dependent upon the temperature of the water. As water temperatures rise, dissolved oxygen levels drop, and as water temperatures fall dissolved oxygen

levels rise. Since all cnidarians need a constant bath of oxygen-rich water, it is therefore best to keep the temperature of your aquarium's water nearer the low end of the acceptable temperature range in order to maintain higher dissolved oxygen levels. Temperatures a little above 80°F are tolerable, but a temperature closer to 75°F is optimal.

You should also keep in mind that while water tem-

paring the weight of a given volume of water to the weight of an equal volume of pure fresh water of the same temperature. As a reference point pure water at room temperature has a specific gravity of 1.000. Therefore an equal volume of water with any dissolved salts or other chemicals in it will be at least slightly heavier and thus will have a higher specific gravity than pure water. The specific gravity of sea water around most coral reefs varies from about 1.022 to 1.030 at 75°F. However, as with temperature, dissolved oxygen levels are also affected by specific gravity. As sea water is made saltier and the specific gravity gets higher, the dissolved oxygen content of the water gets lower (it may be easier to think of the water as being "full of salt" and not leaving much room for oxygen and other gases to dissolve into it), and as specific gravity gets lower dissolved oxygen level increases. For this reason it is also best to keep the specific gravity in your aquarium closer to the lower limit of 1.022 in order to keep oxygen levels as high as possible.

Specific gravity is controlled best when making up artificial sea water to fill the aquarium; it can easily be measured using a device called a hydrometer. Hydrometers are available in different materials and styles, but all are relatively inexpensive. Remember also that the specific gravity of the water in an aquarium will change as the water evaporates. As evaporation occurs, only fresh water evaporates, leaving the salt behind and thus slightly raising the specific gravity of the remain-ing water. (That is why you should never forget to replace evaporated water with fresh water, not salt water!)

SEAWATER pH

The pH of water is a number scale from 0-14 used to describe whether the water is acidic, basic or neutral. Pure water (which is neutral) has a pH of 7. Water with a lower pH is acidic, and water with a higher pH is basic. The pH of sea water around most coral reefs varies from about 8.0 to 8.4, so it is best to maintain a pH of that range in your aquarium. As with temperature, changes in pH must be made slowly.

The pH of aquarium water is to a good extent controlled by the concentration of dissolved carbon dioxide. If CO_2 concentrations are high the pH goes down; when CO_2 concentrations are low the pH rises. It is thus best to keep CO_2 concentrations relatively low. This is usually accomplished in marine aquariums simply by maintaining good water circulation and by keeping the water's surface well agitated to promote good gas exchange between the aquarium and the atmosphere. If this does not keep the pH within acceptable limits the pH can be corrected by using any of a variety of buffers that can be purchased as powders or liquids. Just remember that if you must manually adjust the pH of your aquarium it must be done slowly, over a period of several hours so that no inhabitants are subjected to a "pH shock."

The alkalinity of water is a measure of how well it resists rapid changes in pH. As

Invertebrates like these cnidarians are even more sensitive than fishes are to fluctuations in elements of water quality such as pH and carbonate hardness, as well as the presence or absence of trace elements.

stated, the pH in an aquarium is strongly affected by the concentration of CO_2 in the water. Symbiotic algae inside cnidarians use much of this CO_2 during the day, but at night photosynthesis stops and CO_2 concentrations go up. If the alkalinity is low, the pH can fluctuate a good bit from day to night. Various other conditions that change over time can also have an effect on pH changes. Rapid pH swings can be detrimental to many marine organisms, so alkalinity must be kept within acceptable limits. This is especially true of the stony corals commonly kept in association with soft corals and anemones. There are two basic scales used for the same

method of testing, and values are given in milliequivalents per liter (meq/l) or in carbonate hardness (dKH). For sea water around most coral reefs the alkalinity ranges from 2.1 to 2.5 meq/l or 6 to 7 dKH. However, because aquariums tend to be by nature more unstable than the oceans, the optimum alkalinity should be maintained a little higher than that of sea water. An alkalinity between 2.5 and 3.5 meq/l (7-10 dKH) is optimum for all reef aquarium inhabitants.

ESSENTIAL ELEMENTS

Some substances found in sea water are required by soft corals and anemones but are either not provided in syn-

thetic sea salts or are depleted in the aquarium by biological activity. Unfortunately, there are few, if any, reliable and relatively inexpensive methods for testing the concentrations of these chemicals in sea water. For this reason it is important that you closely follow the manufacturer's directions when using synthetic sea salts. After some time you may become more familiar with the requirements of your reef aquarium and may adjust dosages accordingly, but take caution if or when you do.

Iodine

While normally we all think of oxygen as being a good thing, it is produced in differ-

The clarity of the water in a marine aquarium is only one consideration in determining its status. More important in deciding whether the aquarium's water is good or bad is the question of whether it contains, in sufficient quantity, the elements that corals depend on in their life processes. Photo by U. Erich Friese.

A surge channel at the edge of an Australian reef. Unpolluted natural reef waters are very low in organic nutrients. Photo by Walt Deas.

ent forms during photosynthetic and metabolic processes within corals and anemones. Some forms can be very destructive and must be neutralized within an organism's tissues in order to avoid problematic levels. To combat this potential toxic buildup, corals and anemones use iodine in complex processes to neutralize these forms of oxygen. Iodine is found in several forms in sea water at a concentration of about 60 parts per billion and can be added to the aquarium by using any of a wide variety of prefabricated liquid additives. Again, it is best to simply follow the manufacturer's directions.

Trace Elements

Several other elements found in very low concentrations in sea water are nevertheless important if your corals and anemones are going to thrive. However, because the term "trace elements" includes several different individual elements found in very low concentrations, it also is not practical to test their concentrations in aquarium water. However, most are found in quality salt mixes and can be maintained in sufficient concentrations even if only small water changes are performed regularly. There are also several trace element additives available in liquid form and in blocks that slowly dissolve over a period of days or weeks when placed into the aquarium.

Phosphates

While tiny amounts of phosphate are required by corals, there is basically never any need to add any to the aquarium. In fact, almost without exception reef aquariums have much higher than desirable levels of phosphate, and the hobbyist must constantly try to keep concentrations at a minimum. This is because various forms of phosphate can cause real problems in the aquarium if levels rise to concentrations even as low as 0.1ppm. Monitoring the concentration of phosphate in the aquarium is somewhat troublesome to hobbyists, as it is very difficult to test for. Unfortunately, phosphate comes in both organic and inorganic forms, and most test kits can measure only the inorganic type. While elevated phosphate concentrations may not have a direct detrimental effect on either soft corals or anemones, it is best to do what you can to keep inorganic phosphate below 0.1ppm. Actually, the closer to zero the better,

Algae of various types can be more than just unsightly in a reef aquarium; they can restrict the growth of or even kill corals. Photo by Dr. C. W. Emmens.

because even very low concentrations of phosphate promote the growth of unwanted algae, including hair algae, and this growth is detrimental to other organisms.

Phosphate concentrations are commonly high in tap water, so it is almost always best to use purified water when replacing evaporated aquarium water and when doing water changes. Phosphate also enters the aquarium as an integral part of fish foods, which is a good reason to keep fish populations at a minimum in a reef aquarium. Even if there are only a few fish in your aquarium you should still be

very cautious about overfeeding them. If phosphate is still a problem there are several products that are made to absorb and remove phosphate from the water. Most all of these work very well, but they can also be somewhat expensive if used on a continual basis.

ORGANIC COMPOUNDS AND OTHER IMPURITIES

The removal of surplus organic materials and other unwanted chemicals is also very important. In most aquariums this removal is usually carried out by using activated carbon as a chemical "sponge" because of the

carbon's ability to absorb quite a variety of these compounds. However, activated carbon also sucks up many of the chemicals required by cnidarians to live, including iodine and trace elements, so it should not be used frequently in reef aquariums. Carbon should instead be used periodically, maybe for a few days every two or three months. Specialized filters called protein skimmers are used instead.

Protein skimmers, which are almost always tubular devices, produce a thick foam that can be collected and discarded. There are two basic types of skimmers, venturi driven and airstone driven, but both make a foam by means of producing thousands of tiny air bubbles that are forced into the aquarium water, which is run through the skimmer by means of an external pump or powerhead. Many organic molecules, oils, detergents, etc., have a natural tendency to adhere to the surface of the bubbles and thus can be extracted from the aquarium water by removing the foam. Protein skimmers also aid in the removal of nitrate and phosphates as well and are vital pieces of equipment in the maintenance of high water quality. You should definitely invest in a well made model that is rated for the size of your aquarium.

Both the blue tang (*Acanthurus coeruleus*) shown above and the wrasse (*Bodianus bimaculatus*) shown below are potential contributors of pollutants to the reef aquarium through their production of ammonia and the contribution of phosphates resulting from fish foods. Some fish species also are more directly dangerous because they actively destroy the corals. Photos by Mark Smith.

AMMONIA, NITRITE AND NITRATE

It is well known that fishes and other various organisms in marine aquariums excrete highly toxic ammonia as a waste product of their metabolism. Ammonia is also produced in the aquarium by the decay and breakdown of fish foods, organic matter and dead tissues and can sometimes be found in tap water. Fortunately, two types of bacteria will establish themselves in an aquarium and will convert ammonia to other chemicals. *Nitrosomonas* bacteria use ammonia as a food source

and convert it into nitrite (which is also toxic). Next, *Nitrobacter* bacteria use the nitrite for food and convert it to the far, far less toxic compound nitrate. This conversion process is commonly known as the nitrogen cycle and is the goal of "biological filtration."

In sea water around coral reefs ammonia and nitrite levels are effectively 0 ppm because both substances are consumed as quickly as they are produced. Therefore the optimum concentration of both ammonia and nitrite in the aquarium should always be zero (0 ppm). Special biological filters must be used on most marine (and freshwater) aquariums, which through a variety of methods provide a place for these bacteria to live and multiply. They come in many shapes and types and sizes, the most common being wet-dry filters, undergravel filters and fluidized-bed filters. However, bacteria will also grow on and in the rough natural surfaces of live rock. Therefore, in reef aquariums that have a sufficient amount of live rock, these biological filters are not strictly required. The exact of amount of live rock needed before you can do away with filters is highly variable, depending on how much livestock is added to the aquarium, but somewhere from 1 to 2 pounds of rock per gallon of aquarium volume is usually more than sufficient. However, if much less rock than this is used in the aquarium, or if the aquarium is very well stocked with fishes, additional biological filtration may be required.

After setting up a marine aquarium there is usually a 3- to 5-week period of waiting for the bacteria to multiply and colonize the biological filter. This wait is called the "cycling period" and is normally initiated by adding one or two small fish to the aquarium and nothing else for a while. The fish carry some of the bacteria that will slowly begin to consume the toxins that the fish excrete; the bacteria will multiply until an equilib-

rium is reached between the production and consumption of ammonia. The bacteria are normally slow to multiply, which is why the wait is so long. If live rock is added to the aquarium when it is being set up, the waiting period is typically much shorter. This is due to the fact that the rock may already be heavily colonized with bacteria. So remember that if you use plenty of live rock you might not need extra biological filtration such as provided by wet-drys, and the time it takes to cycle the aquarium will probably be relatively short. However, no matter how you get started you should always try to consult knowledgeable aquarium shop staff or hobbyists and use the appropriate test kits to deter-

mine whether it is safe to begin adding corals to your aquarium.

After all of this is done you are still stuck with the nitrate produced by *Nitrobacter*. There are species of bacteria that use nitrate for food, but they are a different type of bacteria and can only thrive in water with very little dissolved oxygen. For this reason only small amounts of nitrate are consumed deep within the tiny pores and cracks found in pieces of live rock where oxygen levels are lower than in the rest of the aquarium. It is also why nitrate is usually produced faster than it is used up.

Excess nitrate apparently does not have any direct toxic effect on most aquarium inhabitants, but it does have

Live rock in a holding tank at an Australian wholesale establishment. Photo by U. Erich Friese, courtesy JEM Aquatics.

a long-term effect on the pH and alkalinity in the aquarium. That's because nitrate in the aquarium leads to the production of small amounts of nitric acid, which lowers the pH. Periodic partial water changes can reduce the concentration of nitrate if it should become a problem, and protein skimmers can help reduce levels as well.

WATER CLARITY

Aquarium water is usually made cloudy by suspended particles of various sorts that are produced within the aquarium. These particles include feces (whole or broken up), fish foods, dead microorganisms and silt/sediment produced by the natural breakdown of rocks in the aquarium by boring and burrowing organisms. So, other than using live rock for biological filtration and skimmers for chemical filtration, the only other filter needed is a mechanical filter to remove these particles from the aquarium and help keep the water clear.

There are several types of mechanical filters on the market; they use a variety of filter media that can be either cleaned or replaced once they become soiled. One of the most common types of mechanical filter is the "outside box" filter, which hangs off the back of the aquarium and typically contains filter floss, pads or sponges. Many models also come with activated carbon in small bags or in bonded pads and allow room for the addition of a small bag of phosphate remover when needed. Canister filters are another popular mechanical filter. They are typically

constructed from a cylinder with a self-contained pump and filter media. Canister filters are more appealing to some hobbyists, because they usually sit out of sight underneath the aquarium and allow the aquarium to be placed very close to the wall. Many of these filters have specialized baskets or compartments for holding filter floss or sponges and will also hold activated carbon or phosphate remover.

LIGHTING

Lighting is the basic and most important (and commonly the most expensive) difference between "fish-only" marine aquariums and reef aquariums. Because many of the cnidarians that we put

and yellow parts of the spectrum in the first few feet, which is why waters around coral reefs always have a blue color to them unless the water is very shallow. Zooxanthellae have adapted to this situation by being able to specifically use blue light for photosynthetic processes. So the basic idea is to use lights that emit a sufficient amount of blue light to promote photosynthesis. However, a certain amount of white light is also usually desirable over the aquarium so that the tank doesn't look like as if it's full of blue toilet cleanser.

The color of any light can be described in degrees Kelvin (°K). The more towards the yellow and red part of the

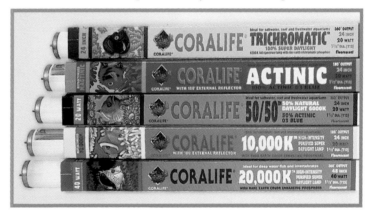

A wide range of fluorescent bulbs is available to provide needed lighting for both shallow and deep tanks in a number of different lighting spectra. Photo courtesy of Energy Savers Unlimited.

into aquariums have photosynthetic zooxanthellae, most require special lighting systems that emit intense light over particular parts of the spectrum. It is therefore vital to purchase a lighting system that produces light of this quality and is sufficiently bright for any of the animals you wish to keep.

Water acts as something of a filter that cuts out the red

spectrum, the lower the Kelvin number and the more towards the blue part the higher the number. While yellowish street lights are usually 4,700°K, actinic (blue) bulbs are around 7,100°K. The optimum color lighting for reef aquariums is around the same as normal daylight or a little bluer, so you should use a lighting system that produces a bright light that is about 6,500°K to 6,800°K.

This can be done in two basic ways. The first and easiest way is to simply buy bulbs that emit light at 6,500°K to 6,800°K. There are currently metal halide bulbs on the market that emit light at exactly 6,500°K, and there are also several brands of fluorescent bulbs that are a mixture of both white and blue light and are appropriately called 50/50 or daylight bulbs. The overall color of these bulbs is usually just a little bluer than daylight and is thus ideal for reef aquariums. The other approach is to use a combination of bulbs of various colors that have an overall emission similar to daylight. This is commonly done by using metal halide bulbs that are 5,500°K with fluorescent bulbs that are 7,100°K. While it is not necessary, many hobbyists also prefer their lighting to actually be even bluer. This is also easily done by combining fluorescent bulbs that are 7,100°K or metal halide bulbs that are 10,000°K with fluorescent bulbs that are 6,500°K.

The other basic consideration is intensity. The right spectrum means little if the intensity is too low. Regular wattage fluorescent bulbs come in a variety of colors from white to actinic-white (50/50) to actinic. However, these bulbs do not have a very high output at all compared with high output (HO) and very high output (VHO) bulbs—but they are much more inexpensive. While some cnidarians can survive with a few of these bulbs over the aquarium, many will require more intense lighting in order

to grow and reproduce. High output and very high output bulbs in these colors are a big step up. While a normal wattage 4-foot fluorescent bulb has an output of 40 watts, a 4-foot HO bulb puts

Experimentation often is needed to find out the best placement for a soft coral within the tank to obtain the proper amount of illumination. This 65-gallon reef aquarium obviously offers different strata of light intensity.

out around 85 watts, and a 4-foot VHO bulb puts out around 110 watts. Compact fluorescents, relatively new to the market, are another type of fluorescent lighting. These bulbs also have a much higher output than regular wattage bulbs, and they are actually a bit brighter than HO and VHO bulbs. Metal halides are by a long shot the

most intense lights available for aquarium applications. They are large bulbs that look just like streetlight bulbs. They also come in a variety of spectrums, from 4,500°K up to 20,000°K. However, the 5,500°K and 6500°K varieties seem to be not only the most reliable but also the cheapest, and as discussed when used in combination with actinic fluorescent bulbs they provide a very desirable spectrum.

Unfortunately, the brighter a particular type of bulb is, the more it usually costs and the more the fixtures and ballasts cost as well. Most manufacturers and hobbyists suggest replacing bulbs every 9 to 18 months depending on the type, so keep in mind the cost of replacing all of your bulbs when deciding on a lighting system. Many of the more intense lighting systems will also get so hot that special cooling fans must be mounted in the canopy or fixture to keep the temperature down.

When it comes to how much your aquarium needs, keep in mind that many soft corals and anemones need at least moderate (HO/VHO/ power compact) and will truly thrive only under intense (metal halide) lighting. For the most part you should try to have the greatest number of bulbs that you can mount over your aquarium without overheating the water (and without breaking you). It's practically impossible to overdo it. Also keep in mind that the deeper your tank is, the less light reaches the organisms nearer the bottom; in general the deeper the tank, the more lighting you'll need.

SELECTING YOUR SPECIMENS

One of the most important factors to take into account when shopping for specimens is the condition of an individual animal offered for sale. Don't buy anything until you've inspected it or them carefully. "Wild" soft corals and anemones are collected almost exclusively in the tropical waters of the South Pacific and are shipped via commercial airlines. To do this, divers must go out onto the reef and carefully (sometimes not carefully enough) collect individual specimens. Some specimens are free-living and are easily gathered, but others are firmly attached to the reef and must be broken away with hammers and chisels. Specimens are then transported to a collection station where they are individually bagged, packed in plastic foam and cardboard boxes, and driven to the local airport. From there most are flown to California, usually Los Angeles, and from there are distributed nationwide. Some suppliers remove the corals from their bags and temporarily place them in holding tanks when they first arrive from the Pacific. The specimens are then re-bagged and re-shipped when they are sold, but some sellers simply rush the corals straight through to stores on the first available flight. The whole trip from collection to store usually takes *at least* 24 hours and often takes as long as 48 hours. Some soft corals and anemones may stay in holding tanks for several days before they are sold, and if conditions are not optimal their health can rapidly decline. The environmental shock of being collected and bagged, as well as the physical stress of flying (rough handling, rapid temperature changes, etc.) often means that when corals and anemones finally arrive at the store many of them may not be in exactly great condition.

Cultivated cnidarians—that is, those not collected from the wilds but propagated and grown domestically in captivity, something that fortunately is being done on an increasingly larger scale—are not subject to the same shipping routines and consequently not to the same shipping stresses. But since you might not be certain of the origin of the specimens

This toadstool leather coral (*Sarcophyton*) has retracted all of its polyps; the raised bumps and pores mark the places from which the polyps normally extend. The fact that a leather coral of a different species (to the left of *Sarcophyton*) is fully expanded while this individual is not may indicate that the *Sarcophyton* is either unhealthy or being irritated by something nearby.

This specimen of a *Litophyton* leather coral is a cutting from a larger individual. It has taken hold of a piece of shell and has been moved from a breeder box into the aquarium—and it's doing very well.

offered to you, when shopping for new livestock you should always be on the lookout for and avoid:

1. *Specimens that have obvious tissue damage*

Tissue damage or decay is usually seen as areas of the specimen's fleshy body that have a moldy or rotten look to them; such a condition is often called tissue necrosis. Dead or damaged flesh is often covered by a nasty brown jelly-like material, while in other cases it is evident only as obvious missing areas of flesh. This condition usually worsens over a short period of time and can lead to the death of an individual or sometimes a whole colony. An exception is in cases where a specimen has a lesion in a location that can be carefully pruned. If this is the case, the damaged or dead portions can sometimes be carefully broken away or cut off without any damage to the rest of the animal.

2. *Specimens that have bleached*

A bleached specimen in effect has lost most or all of its zooxanthellae. This is a common side effect of the organism's getting too hot during shipping, but it can be caused also by other factors such as exposure to excessive UV radiation or from a lack of intense light. In the wild, affected corals are sometimes repopulated by zooxanthellae relatively quickly and survive, but they typically do not recover in aquariums.

3. *Specimens that are not expanded*

Specimens that are normally covered with polyps may retract somewhat at night, but if they fail to expand or "polyp out" over a few days' time they are more than likely irritated or unhealthy. Many soft corals will be shrunken and retracted if this is the case. Likewise, anemones commonly close up at night but should reopen soon after the lights are turned on. If an anemone fails to do so it also is probably irritated or unhealthy. It is unwise to purchase any such specimen that fails to open fully.

THE INDIVIDUAL GROUPS

The following sections are intended to provide you with specific information about many of the soft corals and anemones commonly seen for sale in aquarium stores. While in the past it seemed that wholesalers and retailers had made up their own names for each individual cnidarian group, today almost all have one somewhat universal common name. In the pages that follow, various soft corals, anemones, and other related cnidarians are referred to by these individual common names. For many the generic name (the capitalized first name of the two names in today's binomial system of nomenclature) is provided as well, but the specific name (the uncapitalized second half of a scientific name) is usually not provided, because when dealing with soft corals it is almost never used due to the great difficulty involved in proper identification. Also keep in mind that many soft corals that are very similar in appearance may share a common name but are actually members of more than one genus or can be different species of the same genus.

For each group of organisms some basic information is given to explain a little about them and to help you choose which ones to stock your aquarium with. When it is needed, other more specific information is also provided. General lighting requirements and overall hardiness and aggressiveness levels are given where applicable. However, you should keep in mind that these are general guidelines and are greatly dependent on the water quality in your aquarium and the dealer's aquariums, how various specimens tolerate shipping at different times of the year, how and where they are collected from and other pertinent factors.

Where lighting is discussed, remember that various lighting systems are considered to be low output, moderate output, or intense output. For general purposes several regular wattage fluorescent bulbs (4 to 6) over aquariums from 18 to 24 inches deep (most aquariums from 55 to 150 gallons) is considered low output, even if actinic bulbs are included. Moderate lighting output over the same aquariums requires the use of several VHO fluorescent bulbs or compact-type bulbs. To achieve intense lighting over the same aquariums requires the use of metal halide systems, usually with a combination of fluorescent bulbs. Of course you must keep in mind that a system that is considered to be moderate over an aquarium that is 20 inches deep would be considered intense over an aquarium

Leather corals, zoanthids, corallimorphs and other cnidarians are represented in this 60-gallon reef tank.

27

only 12 inches deep and would be considered low over an aquarium that is 36 inches deep. The depth (distance from the bulbs) at which a specimen is placed in the aquarium is affected the same way. A specimen that requires only moderate lighting may thrive at the very bottom of a deep aquarium with an intense lighting system, while one that requires intense light may need to be placed very near the top of the aquarium. Try to use good common sense when choosing specimens according to your own lighting system and where you plan to place each.

Where current preferences are discussed they are typically more straightforward. Many specimens actually prefer to be placed in areas of low current and should be placed where there is little water movement or they commonly will not expand fully. The majority of specimens will do fine with a moderate current. They should be placed in an area where there is considerable water movement, but not in a direct current from a powerhead or other pump return. Lastly, specimens that actually thrive in a strong current should be placed where they are directly blown upon by currents from powerheads or other pumps.

Many specimens are injured during collection and die during the trip to the pet store or shortly after. For this reason the information concerning the hardiness of different specimens is a guide of how well they commonly fare in the aquarium *if* they are unharmed after shipping, or if they go on to survive any problems. In other words, just because you might see a shipment come in with several dead or dying individuals does not mean that they are particularly fragile or not hardy. They may simply have had an unusually bad trip, and other similar specimens may be fine for the aquarium.

The aggressiveness of different specimens is affected by several factors. Some are considered to be non-aggressive and can be placed very near, or even in direct contact with, others. In many cases you should be more worried about their being victims instead of aggressors. However, as discussed earlier, many cnidarians, such as anemones, have stinging tentacles that can be employed in order to damage or kill unwanted neighbors. Also remember that many soft corals exude invisible poisons that can damage or even kill nearby neighbors.

Although the soft corals in this photo (a *Cladiella* species, commonly called a colt coral, is featured most prominently) can bother each other they tend to have little if any effect on stony corals (such as the stony coral *Scolymia* species to the right of *Cladiella*) and can be placed very near them with no danger to the stony coral. It is much more common for the stony coral to be the aggressor, using stinging tentacles to injure or kill.

ORDER ALCYONACEA:
THE LEATHER CORALS

There are several types of alcyonaceans, and most are typically referred to as leather corals. As the name implies, some leather corals tend to be somewhat tough to the touch and have a texture much like that of wet leather. Still others, while being closely related, have a much softer feel and are somewhat "squishy" to the touch. Leather corals are very common in various reef environments and are found in quite a variety of shapes and colors; many individuals of this group can reach sizes of a few feet across. They often have to be pruned like bushes to keep them from growing out of the aquarium when kept under intense lighting!

Incidentally, we'll have to get something straight about common names, or at least the names used for the various cnidarian groups covered in this publication, right now. If not, there's going to be a lot more confusion than needed. There certainly is enough confusion surrounding the identification of cnidarian animals in general without causing more by not having an agreed-upon basis of understanding for the names being used in the text. The basic problem probably derives from the use of the word "coral" as part of the common names of groups that are very widely separated taxonomically. For example, you have the cnidarians to which the common name "fire corals" is applied, even though the "fire corals" are not even within the same taxonomic class as the reef-building animals generally thought of when the word "corals" comes up. (The fire corals are within the class Hydrozoa and the reef-building corals within the class Anthozoa.) Now the distinc- tions between taxa at the class level are supposed to be very large indeed—birds are in one class and mammals in a different class, for example, and birds and mammals are pretty different from one another, aren't they?—so if you're trying to avoid confu- sion it's probably unwise to link the fire corals and the

Closeup of the very slender polyps and the tiny light-colored tips of a very large (about 15 inches in diameter) leather coral of the genus _Sarcophyton_.

reef-building corals semantically through use of a word shared by both common names.

The problem, though, is that where common names truly serve the purpose of identifying particular animals and groups of animals because the names are actually used by people who deal with the animals (as opposed to so-called "common" or "popular" names that are simply coined for the purpose of creating a non-scientific name because the scientifc name is assumed to be too hard to learn) we're pretty much stuck with them.

And that's why the general term "soft corals" is used to apply to not only the members

Fishes, crabs, shrimp and other dwellers of the reef may occasionally it on or crawl across a leather coral, and individual corals react differently to such intrusions. The small blue-leg hermit crab shown in the photo below has obviously irritated the toadstool leather coral on which it's perched, because the coral has retracted all of its polyps. Conversely, in the photo above a large bicolor blenny has decided to use the top of the toadstool leather coral as a perch with no reaction at all from the coral. The fish shown often sits atop the coral in the photo, so the coral may have become acclimated to the contact.

of the order Alcyonacea within the subclass Octocorallia of the class Anthozoa but also to such disparate groups as the gorgonians (order Gorgonacea), the star polyps (order Stolonifera, which happens also to be the order that contains the organ pipe "corals," another group with "coral" in its name even though it's not in even the same subclass as the reef-building corals), the zoanthids (order Zoanthidea), the corallimorphs (order Corallimorpharia) and the "true" anemones (order Actiniaria). The last-named

scientifically precise and isn't very descriptive, but it's very commonly used in the aquarium trade and hobby.

Even using the term "reef-building" in reference to the "true" corals— members of the Order Scleractinia in the subclass Hexacorallia— does not provide enough contradistinction between groups, because some other cnidarians (the blue "coral" *Heliopora*, which isn't even in the same subclass as the scleractinians, is an example) build structures that could easily be considered to be small reefs; additionally, there also are some "true corals" that don't build reefs, so the term is misleading on both exclusionary and inclusionary counts.

Even marine biologists have trouble identifying many alcyonaceans at the species

The thickly branched shape of these (*Sinularia* species) corals' bodies makes it easy to see why they are often called "finger leathers."

level, and most simply don't try. Many of these animals are so similar in appearance and structure that they can be identified only at the generic level—and in many cases not even then. The most reliable method of identification is to collect skeletal fragments in the form of sclerites and spicules from a specimen. These fragments, while being very small, are usually unique enough in structure to aid in classification. But obviously it is not an option for most hobbyists (or collectors, or dealers), so most of the leather corals are sorted and sold by common name only.

Alcyonaceans have fleshy stems that are reinforced structurally by tiny carbonate sclerites. These are small spiny structures (usually only a millimeter or two in length) that are made of the same material that stony corals use to form their skeletons. The sclerites are meshed together within the coral's tissues like puzzle pieces to form a sort of pseudo-skeleton that can be somewhat rigid to very flexible. Different types of corals

A leather coral of the genus *Sarcophyton,* showing the mushroom-shaped body that has given rise to the common name of "toadstool" corals; they are also sometimes called "umbrella leathers."

three orders at least are in the same subclass as the reef-building corals, so they are considerably different taxonomically from the other animals being lumped together here as "soft corals." The designation certainly isn't very

A *Sinularia* species with the "fingers" tightly clumped.

Above and below: two of the several different types of leather corals belonging to the genus *Sarcophyton,* showing variation in the length and density of the polyps as well as the basic shapes of the animals. Different species in this genus also come in different colors and have varying degrees of "ruffles" where the upper portion of the body takes on a folded shape.

use different types of these structures and utilize different arrangements of them according to how "tough" they need to be. All of these animals also utilize a strong base to stay affixed to the bottom; they cannot be removed from the base without serious effort. That is why almost all are imported pre-attached to small pieces of live rock.

They are all also covered with numerous tiny pores from which small individual polyps can expand. Each polyp has eight tentacles and in many cases they are pinnate, meaning that the tentacles themselves are covered with smaller tentacles. The expansion of the polyps is commonly called "polyping out" by hobbyists and is easy to observe as the corals react to aquarium lights being turned on in the morning. It is

A very large—almost two feet across!—*Sinularia.*

common to see these polyps fully expanded during the day and then completely retracted at night, but you should take note of corals that keep their polyps retracted for more than a day or two, indicating that they are probably unhealthy, irritated or just unhappy. All of these animals are typically very hardy, and if this behavior is noticed it can commonly

Cuttings from a *Sinularia* (below) and *Litophyton* (right) that have adhered to pieces of rock or shell while in a breeder box and have now been positioned in an aquarium, where they are growing successfully.

Above left: closeup of a branch of a colt coral (*Cladiella*), illustrating how some of the polyps can be very finely branched, almost feathery, in appearance. Above right: a large colt coral in a 75-gallon aquarium. This individual grew from about six inches across to over a foot across in less than a year under a combination of metal halide and fluorescent lighting. Colt corals can reach even greater sizes than that relatively quickly when exposed to intense lighting.

be remedied simply by moving the leather coral to a different location in the aquarium. Moving the individual not only gets it away from possible irritating neighbors but also usually moves it into a different current. In some instances just the change of current is sufficient to entice a leather coral to polyp out.

All leather corals enjoy at least a moderate current. In fact, many of the branching forms like a very strong direct current and will not thrive in anything less. Sometimes the process of finding a spot that they like may take more than a couple of tries.

Both the leather corals and many other alcyonaceans contain zooxanthellae and do not require any sort of feeding. However, they do enjoy strong illumination in the aquarium. Many species will grow several inches in one year if kept under metal halide lighting. Conversely,

most will also survive with much less intense lighting, such as setups using several normal wattage fluorescent bulbs or a few high-output fluorescent bulbs. However, they tend to grow less quickly, if at all, under these lights. If you do place one of these leather corals under metal

This closeup photo of a *Sinularia* species shows how dense the polyp cover can be on some leather corals; this particular individual has so many polyps it looks fuzzy.

halide lighting it is usually a good idea to give them a few days to a couple of weeks to slowly become acclimated to such intensity. Try only leaving the lights on for a few hours a day, each day leaving them on a little longer. Alternatively, at first place the coral near the bottom of the aquarium and then move it up closer to the surface a step at a time.

While leather corals require calcium and strontium to build sclerites in their bodies, both of these elements are usually found in sufficient quantities in the aquarium water if periodic water changes are performed. If, however, other organisms in the aquarium also use these elements it may be necessary to add small doses of each. About the only other additive that they require is some source of iodine, which should be added on a regular basis to ensure that your specimens will stay healthy and grow. They may also fare better with the use of small trace element additions.

Some alcyonaceans do require feeding. The leather corals commonly called carnation corals, genus *Dendronephthya*, are prime examples. These animals are very attractive and come in a splendor of colors when seen in stores, but they almost without exception do not fare well in aquariums. They require frequent feedings of tiny plankton to stay healthy and should be avoided unless painstaking attention will be paid to their needs.

Like many other cnidarians, the alcyonaceans defend their "territory" on the reef by means of alleopathy. This is the use of various chemicals that can weaken nearby cnidarian animals and inhibit their growth, thus leaving more room for the defender to grow. There are a variety of compounds used,

Members of the genus *Nephthea* are commonly called "tree leathers" because of their relatively thick central stalks and bushy tops.

Dendronephthya, one of the carnation corals, a group that requires special care.

but most are terpenoids. Others are diterpenoids, sarcophines and other compounds that are commonly used for the same purpose by plants. These compounds can have a very strong effect on cnidarians within a few inches, but they can also have lessened yet noticeable negative effects farther away if the affected animals are down-current. In this case, the alcyonacean producing the toxin is giving the down-current recipient a weak but constant bath of toxins. If you suspect this is happening in your aquarium, try to move individual specimens around

to different locations. In extreme cases even this may not help, and certain animals may have to be removed from the aquarium. It can be extremely difficult trying to determine exactly which cnidarian is the culprit in a reef aquarium with strong multidirectional currents!

Another interesting tidbit about leather corals is that they are very easy to propagate in the aquarium. Almost any of them can be carefully pruned to grow small new individuals. When this is done the parent leather coral will heal relatively quickly, and the clipping can attach itself

A small *Xenia* colony. The stalks of these polyps are very thin and elongated, and the tentacles of each polyp are elongated as well. While it appears that this alcyonacean could easily capture prey with its tentacles, *Xenia* species in fact do not take any solid foods at all. All nutrients required are derived from zooxanthellae or absorbed directly from sea water.

Species of the genus *Xenia* are among the most interesting alcyonaceans. When expanded fully from their base the polyps of a *Xenia* colony enjoy a moderate to strong current and will wave freely; some species also exhibit a "pulsing" motion as the polyps rapidly open and shut their tentacles as if they were trying to breathe or swim. In some individuals this pulsing motion stops permanently for unknown reasons. Photo by Walt Deas.

to a piece of rock within a few days. To do this simply cut away a piece of the top of a toadstool-type leather coral or a branch of another alcyonacean using a razor blade. The parent should then be placed under strong current to ensure that the cut area stays clean and free of detritus. The cutting should be placed in an area of lower current with some small pieces of live rock to act as a new foothold. One very effective method is purchasing a "breeder box," which is usually used to separate baby fish from larger fish in freshwater

An example of a toadstool leather coral undergoing reproduction by budding. Budding typically occurs as large buds grow from the base of a toadstool leather coral (seen here only as a stalk) and then continue to grow into full-sized corals. It is very easy to take advantage of this occurrence by simply snipping off the buds, letting them attach to a new piece of rock and then moving them to a more desirable location.

This small leather coral has grown from a very small cutting that had been plugged into a hole in the top of a piece of live rock. The process worked well for this particular specimen because the rock is flat-topped and has several deep holes in it; also, the current in the rock's area is relatively low.

aquariums. One of these boxes can be hung inside the aquarium with the bottom covered with small bits of live rock. The cutting(s) can be placed inside and should settle onto the bottom. After 7 to 14 days the cuttings will usually take hold of one of the pieces of live rock and can

then be moved out of the box and placed wherever is desirable in the aquarium. Other times small cuttings can be shoved into holes in live rock where the fit is tight enough to keep them from being blown away by strong currents. This can be more difficult than it sounds, however, because leather corals tend to shrink and expand their tissues. A cutting that seems to fit snugly within a hole may eventually shrink itself to the point that it falls out of the hole and gets blown away. If you try this method, be sure to keep a close watch on the cutting's progress.

Many leather corals periodically form an unusual-looking waxy coating over their bodies. This coating

usually covers most of the animal, but it is especially thick upon the tops of leather corals that have flattened or cup-like upper bodies. The coating is eventually sloughed away after a few days, and it is thought that the sloughing is a mechanism for the removal of any detritus that has settled on top or of microalgae that are trying to grow on the upper portion, where most sunlight is received. While in most cases this seems to be a harmless process, on occasion it has been observed that the wax can strongly irritate other cnidarians that it may come to settle on in the aquarium. So it is a good idea to watch closely to see whether a leather coral begins to shed its waxy coat; that way you can remove any bits

Left: This finger leather coral had retracted its polyps and formed a thin wax coat over its entire body. The coat eventually peeled away after about three days, and the polyps then immediately expanded.

and pieces large enough to collect.

Also note that if a leather coral does wax over, but does not shed its coat within a few days, the lack of shedding may be a sign that the animal is irritated. This is a common occurrence in unhealthy leather corals, leather corals that are being physically or chemically attacked by others and leather corals that are not receiving enough current across their surfaces to remove any accumulation of detritus.

This toadstool leather coral is in the process of preparing to discard a waxy coat that had formed on it three days earlier. The polyps (which had been retracted since the formation of the wax coat) are expanding underneath the coat and will help to force the coat away from the body.

ORDER GORGONACEA:
THE SEA FANS AND SEA WHIPS

The various members of the order Gorgonacea are commonly called gorgonians by aquarium hobbyists but are also known as sea fans, sea whips, sea rods or sea blades to others. These cnidarian animals can reach sizes of several feet across in the wild but are usually collected at a much smaller size. Like the true corals, the gorgonians also are colonial cnidarians, but they are somewhat different in structure from any of the hard corals and their closer kin. Each gorgonian consists of hundreds or thousands of polyps that produce a branching skeleton composed of a protein called gorgonin. This skeleton is exceptionally tough yet somewhat flexible, and it is reinforced with layers of carbonate sclerites. Around the skeleton is wrapped the fleshy portion of the animal, which varies greatly in color and thickness. The overall shape of a gorgonian can range from a finely branching plume-like form to a flattened almost

This photo illustrates an advantage that gorgonians have over many other alcyonaceans: other corals are very close by, but the gorgonians ((Leptogorgia featured most prominently) don't appear to be bothered by them—and they don't appear to be bothering the other corals, making the gorgonians ideal for crowded aquaria.

mesh-like form; on each form the polyps are found to line the entire surface of the branches. The whole of the animal is firmly attached to the substrate by a large sturdy base composed of gorgonin, which is nearly impossible to detach. For this reason almost all gorgonians are sold already attached to the piece of live rock they were collected on.

In recent years the collection of corals from the Gulf of Mexico and the Caribbean has been outlawed. However, since gorgonians are abundant in these waters and are not true corals, many of the gorgonians seen currently in aquarium stores are from the Caribbean. But the collection of gorgonians involves the collection of the live rock

Above and below: various gorgonians (a specimen of a gorgonian of the genus _Eunicea_ shown above) among other soft corals, with all of them living in harmony.

pieces that they are attached to, and it happens that the collection of live rock also was banned, resulting in the necessity for chiseling the gorgonians off whatever they were attached to. Obviously this practice commonly produces specimens that have injured bases of attachment, giving potential purchasers a good reason to look carefully before they buy. If a specimen has been collected properly it is quite simple to use an aquarium-safe epoxy cement to glue it to a new piece of live rock or shell in the aquarium.

The branches of the gorgonians are covered with flesh that is riddled with tiny pores from which the polyps can expand for feeding or contract into at night or if disturbed. Each of the polyps has eight tentacles that are covered with smaller branches, called pinnules; the tentacles can vary greatly in size from species to species. In most cases they are at least a few millimeters across. Gorgonians can be placed in the aquarium just about anywhere that a constant moderate to strong current of water passes over their bodies. They do not seem to exude any toxic substances that irritate nearby neighbors and do not possess any type of poisonous tentacles. However, they should not be placed where stony corals or anemones can give them a sting.

Gorgonians are filter feeders that capture floating plankton. Many are also photosynthetic and will require moderate to intense lighting to thrive. However, while the photosynthetic varieties have colored polyps, there are a few available species that have colorless or white polyps, indicating a lack of zooxanthellae; these gorgonians can be kept under just about any lighting conditions. One thing to keep in mind is that in the aquarium there is very little if any plankton for filter feeders to eat. This is not a problem for the photosynthetic varieties of gorgonians if they are kept in a well lit aquarium, but those that are not photosynthetic will commonly require being fed regularly to stay healthy. To do this, most species of both the photsynthetic and non-photosynthetic gorgonians can be given a meal of baby brine shrimp or other plankton-like food using an eyedropper. Simply squirt a water-and-food mixture over the gorgonian's open polyps and watch them gobble up all they can catch.

As you shop for a gorgonian, be sure to inspect it for any obvious damage and also take a close look to see whether any of its skeleton is exposed. The skeleton will have a brown or black color and should not be visible if the gorgonian is completely healthy. If the skeleton is exposed anywhere it is an indication that some area of the gorgonian's tissues have died and sloughed away. This is commonplace due to lack a proper handling techniques.

Gorgonians should never be exposed to air. They should go from the reef to your tank without ever being exposed to air for even just a few seconds. They are extremely sensitive to exposure, and

A gorgonian of the genus *Briareum*, commonly referred to as an encrusting gorgonian. *Briareum* does not form a branching structure but instead usually overgrows other gorgonian species, using them as a support. The individual shown here is taking over a non-photosynthetic gorgonian known as a sea whip. Unfortunately the encruster usually completely covers the encrustee and causes its death, but the *Briareum* lives on and provides the hobbyist with a beautiful specimen.

Known as the red sea spray, this *Leptogorgia* individual has lost some of the live tissue on its branches. The depletion is seen where a few inches of the tough brown skeleton are exposed at the ends of some of the branches. Gorgonians that show such areas should be avoided, as the condition commonly spreads down the branches and leads to the demise of the entire animal.

their tissues will usually die if exposure occurs. To avoid this, make sure the specimen is put into a bag that is *full* of water when purchased. There should be no air in the bag at all. Then, when placing the specimen into your aquarium, put the whole bag into the water and open it below the surface so that the gorgonian can be removed without risk.

Unfortunately, even if specimens are handled correctly and given the right conditions in the aquarium they still tend to be only moderately hardy at best. In fact, gorgonians are probably on the whole the most difficult of all of the" soft corals" to keep for long periods of time. In some cases they will live apparently happily for several months or even a couple of years, then wither away and die. Very few hobbyists can get a gorgonian to live for more than three or four years.

As far as reproduction in the aquarium goes, on rare occasions it has been seen that gorgonians can drop off small portions of their branches. This may be an unusual, or even accidental, method of reproduction, but it does happen. If you should see this happening in your aquarium, you can pick up the pieces and stick them into a piece of live rock; if conditions are right, a new gorgonian will start to grow. While it is not advisable, propagation can be attempted by using the same method. Sharp scissors can be used to snip off the end of a branch of a gorgonian, and the snippet can subsequently be stuck into a piece of live rock. Sometimes this will work and the cutting will grow from the rock, but more often than not it will die.

This gorgonian and others of the genus *Eunicea* are known as "candelabras" because of their branching (and often curled) appearance.

ORDER STOLONIFERA: THE STAR POLYPS

Star polyps are another very hardy type of cnidarian readily available to hobbyists. Their stalks are very thin, and even with tentacles fully expanded a polyp may be only a quarter of an inch in diameter. The polyps are also easily distinguished from those of other small encrusting octocorallians because they lack a noticeable mouth. All that is present is what could be called at best a pore. Needless to say, they do not take prepared foods. Star polyps contain zooxanthellae and will grow best under moderate to intense lighting, but they will fare well in the aquarium only if regular additions of an iodine supplement are provided.

Star polyps form colonies of numerous tightly spaced individuals; they are never

Below and above right: green star polyps (genus *Clavularia*) , the star polyps most often available to hobbyists. The colony shown at right is of a very unusual variety.

As seen here, colonies of star polyps will encrust just about any surface available; this colony of brown star polyps is growing up the back glass of the aquarium. It is very easy to cut or peel away such growth and move it to another location in the aquarium simply by wrapping the "sheet" around a piece of live rock or shell. The colony will adhere to the new substrate in a few days and will then continue to grow wherever it is moved.

found as solitary individuals. The common base of attachment that they share is somewhat rubbery in texture and also grows over the substrate in an encrusting manner. Star polyps also have the ability to completely withdraw into their base. The polyps can quickly pull themselves in, looking like rapidly deflating balloons if they are ever disturbed or are irritated, and all that can be seen of them when withdrawn are small pimples on the surface of the base. While they often retreat when disturbed by a fish or motile invertebrate, they do not seem to be bothered by and are not aggressive towards other neighbors.

Propagation of star polyps is easily performed by using sharp scissors or a razor blade to snip off any part of the thick encrusting mat that they form as a base. The clippings can be stuck into holes in pieces of live rock or can be wrapped onto a piece of live rock and secured with a small rubber band. New polyps will begin to grow from the mat after a couple of weeks under good conditions and will quickly begin to spread over the surrounding area.

Brown star polyps; like the green star polyps, the brown stars also are in the genus *Clavularia*.

The glowing green color of these green star polyps is highly iridescent under actinic light, making them a very attractive addition to any reef aquarium using such lighting. The combination shown in this photo of lush green frills set around contrasting blues makes it easy to understand why many people refer to the soft corals in general as "flower animals."

ORDER ZOANTHIDEA:
THE COLONIAL ANEMONES

The order Zoanthidea is composed of two major groups of hexacorallians, the button polyps and sea mats, all of which are commonly called colonial "anemones." As opposed to many of the other types of soft-bodied cnidarians, the largest of the zoanthids reach a length of only a few inches and typically form large encrusting colonies that overgrow rocks and other hard surfaces on the reef.

The button polyps and sea mats are very common in reef aquariums and are some of the hardiest cnidarians available to hobbyists. Each individual polyp is similar to a stalked anemone and has a single centrally located mouth encircled by a ring of small tentacles. The polyps are usually only a quarter of an inch to one inch in size and are secured firmly to the bottom by a fleshy base. While at times some of the various species have polyps that live as solitary animals, many types can also be found in small clusters that are attached together by a common base or by thin strands of flesh. All reproduce by forming smaller clones on the fringes of a colony. In some cases the newer polyps break away from each other and very slowly move to a nearby new location.

All of the button polyps and sea mats have symbiotic zooxanthellae and will grow and reproduce under moderate to intense lighting. Many (but not all) will also take in small food particles and can be fed by using an eyedropper filled with water and prepared foods such as brine shrimp, blood worms, bits of clam

Sun polyps of the genus *Palythoa*. These colonial anemones are usually much larger than any of the other button polyps, sometimes growing to one and a half inches in diameter and three inches in height. They can be fed prepared foods and will grow and multiply quickly in the aquarium under good conditions.

Colonial anemones of the genera *Palythoa* (above) and *Zoanthus* (below), referred to variously as button polyps and sea mats. The distinction between the two depends on whether the individual polyps are connected or unconnected in the colony. While this is usually very difficult to determine without close inspection, the sea mats typically form a tough, fibrous encrusting base from which the polyps grow, whereas in many cases the button polyps can be free-living but closely spaced individual polyps. In the aquarium trade both names seem to be somewhat interchangeable—probably because of the difficulty in telling the two types apart—and members of each group often are sold as the other. The sea mats and button polyps belong to either *Palythoa* or *Zoanthus*; *Palythoa* species are somewhat larger and have larger tentacles and mouths, and most of them will take prepared foods. *Zoanthus* species tend to be smaller and have a less defined mouth, which typically appears to be nothing more than a small centrally situated bump; they do not take prepared foods.

meat, etc. The feeding process is interesting to watch, and the foods help the polyps to grow at a faster rate and reproduce. A good iodine supplement should also be used to encourage growth and reproduction.

Button polyps and sea mats are not aggressive towards their neighbors. They have short tentacles but do not seem to have any ability to sting. The tentacles are more for entrapment of food particles. They will spread over live rock in the reef aquarium and can grow in direct contact with most other cnidarians..

Under favorable conditions and moderate to intense lighting, zoanthids can grow very quickly and live for years in the aquarium. In fact, they commonly have to be pruned back or scraped off rocks to keep them from overtaking the entire tank and overrunning other animals in

Above: A colony of *Palythoa* that almost entirely covers the rock to which it is attached.

Below: A colony of *Parazoanthus*, commonly called yellow polyps. These polyps readily take prepared foods, which they can grab with their long tentacles.

the process. However, if conditions are not satisfactory they are prone to experience a "crash." This occurs when many of them, or all of them in the whole aquarium, die within a very short time span. This die-off can actually occur over a period of just a few hours and can cause serious problems for the hobbyist if a quick cleanup and water change are not performed. It is mandatory to provide adequate iodine additions to the aquarium to ensure that no crash occurs.

Propagation of zoanthids is easily done with a little patience. To spread new colonies around the aquarium or into another aquarium, place small pieces of live rock or seashell in direct contact with an established colony. Within a few weeks the colony should start to grow over the smaller piece of substrate, which can be pulled away from the colony and moved to a new location.

Right and below: both of these photos demonstrate the general lack of any aggression between the various colonial anemones shown. At right a large mushroom anemone is completely surrounded by polyps with no obvious ill effects. In the photo below, *Palythoa* and *Zoanthus* polyps are in direct contact with each other, with no damage to either.

Above and below: typical examples of mushroom anemones of the genus *Discosoma,* commonly called *Actinodiscus* by some hobbyists. The ones shown above exhibit a smooth disk and often show a color that gives them the easy-to-remember common name of red mushrooms. The stripes on the ones shown below have given rise to the descriptive common name of watermelon mushrooms.

ORDER CORALLIMORPHARIA: THE MUSHROOM ANEMONES

Mushroom anemones are solitary polyps that belong to the order Corallimorpharia in the subclass Hexacorallia. This group is made up of several genera, but only four are popular in the aquarium hobby: *Discosoma, Rhodactis, Ricordea* and *Amplexidiscus*. The fact that many of these animals are separated only by their color makes classification very difficult within some of these genera, and the use of species names is rare.

All of the corallimorphs are very similar to both the true anemones and the stony corals, sharing anatomical and physiological characteristics with both, which is why they are sometimes referred to as "coral anemones." Like most other sedentary cnidarians, the mushroom anemones are very simple in design. They attach to the substrate with a short fleshy base and have a thin disk with or without tentacles.

Most are circular or ovoid in shape and have a centrally situated mouth that leads to a gastrovascular cavity where food is digested. Some are completely smooth, but many are rough or fuzzy, and still others may be completely covered with complex tentacles. Although all have zooxanthellae, many of them can be fed prepared foods. Reproduction is commonly by fission, during which the disk of a polyp splits down the

The mushroom anemones of the genus *Discosoma* are very difficult to identify at the specific level, because so many of them are outwardly identical except as regards their color. The question then always becomes: are they actually different species, or are they simply different color variations of the same species? Systematists continue to debate mushroom anemones' taxonomic status.

Discosoma species are relatively smooth or have small bumps or "pimples" that are rudimentary tentacles. Most *Discosoma* can reach a size of three inches or so in diameter under good conditions.

A view illustrating the compatibility of mushroom anemones belonging to the same genus. Members of the genus *Discosoma* can grow close to or even in direct contact with other *Discosoma*. It is common to have several species growing together on the same piece of rock.

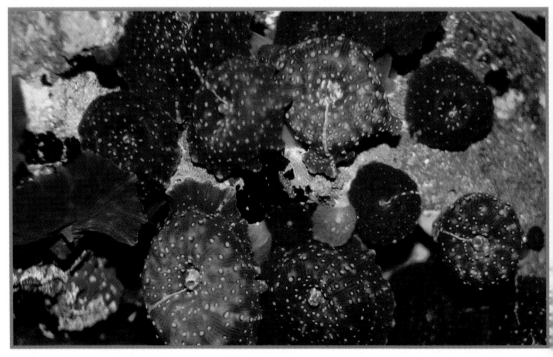

middle into two smaller individuals. In many cases mushroom anemones also reproduce by pedal laceration: the polyp moves over the surface of a rock and leaves behind tiny pieces of its base, each of which will grow into a full-size adult relatively quickly.

Of all the non-scleractinian "corals" available to hobbyists, the mushroom anemones are by far the easiest to care for, because even though they all contain zooxanthellae, almost all will tolerate much lower lighting levels than other photosynthetic cnidarians. In fact, many will do fine in what would be considered the darkest parts of any reef aquarium, where they are shaded or receive only indirect light. Many types actually prefer lower light levels and will shrink and stop reproduction if exposed to intense lights such as metal halides. This

A hairy mushroom anemone in the act of feeding. When these mushrooms eat they close up by rapidly drawing in the edge of their disk; the action is very similar to closing a sack with a drawstring. Once a small bit of food is trapped inside, the mushroom opens its mouth and releases digestive filaments (acontia) from its gastrovascular cavity. The digestive filaments quickly begin to envenom and digest the victim.

Left: A mushroom anemone of the genus *Rhodactis,* typically called bullseye mushrooms and imported on pieces of live rock.

tolerance varies from species to species, however, and when trying to determine what amount of light is best for a particular type you may have to resort to simple experimentation. Start at the bottom of the aquarium and over a period of several days move a colony upward toward the light in the aquarium and watch the results. If the mushrooms expand more fully, keep trying to move them up. If they contract and do not re-

that they come into direct contact with. It is best to keep a close watch on a colony for a while if they are placed very near other inhabitants.

Mushroom anemones can be easily propagated in the aquarium. All that the procedure consists of is taking a colony out of the aquarium and splitting the individual mushrooms down the middle with a razor blade. After placing the colony back into the aquarium the mushrooms will heal very quickly, and each half will grow into a new individual. This technique can be done over and over as long as the halves are well healed before they are re-cut. By using this method you can quickly multiply the number of mushrooms growing on a piece of live rock, and they can eventually spread out over more of the aquarium.

Rhodactis species, which can reach sizes of five inches in diameter, are usually called hairy mushrooms because of the digestive tentacles that cover the entire disk. These tentacles, typically branched in a complex manner, are clearly visible. They contain nematocysts, and *Rhodactis* can capture small invertebrates and other foods. They accept prepared foods in the aquarium and will grow and reproduce more quickly if fed on a regular basis.

expand within a couple of days, leave them in lower light.

While many of the large members of the genus *Rhodactis* and the genus *Amplexidiscus* will gladly take prepared foods, almost none of the remaining species need any sort of food whatsoever. They assimilate all the nutrients they require from their zooxanthellae, by absorbing them directly from sea water and by eating bacteria. A good iodine supplement should be added on a regular basis regardless of whether the mushroom anemones eat or not.

Most of the mushrooms are relatively harmless, but others can be quite deadly. Those that have longer tentacles can deliver a strong sting to nearby animals, and a few others that have no tentacles at all still seem to burn other cnidarians

This particular type of hairy mushroom is called a metallic mushroom and fluoresces brilliantly under actinic lighting. Metallic mushrooms are probably the largest of the hairy mushrooms available to hobbyists, often growing to eight to ten inches in diameter.

Above, left and right: examples of mushroom anemones of the genus *Ricordea.* They can be distinguished from other mushroom anemones by the presence of numerous bubble-like tentacles covering their entire disk. They take prepared foods and will reproduce more readily when fed——but even when well fed they still reach a size of only one or two inches in aquaria.

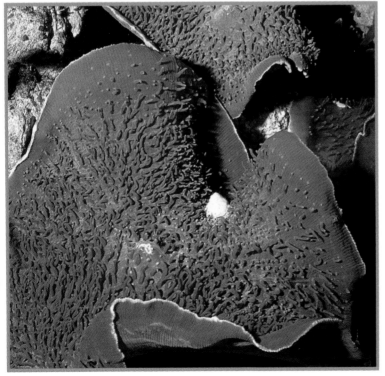

Unlike other types of mushroom anemones, which are almost always found in large colonies, the corallimorphs of the genus *Amplexidiscus* are oten found as solitary individuals or in small groups of four or five. They generally reach larger sizes than cther mushrooms and can be as large as twelve inches in diameter, which has resulted in their common name of elephant ears. Small simple tentacles can be found scattered over their disks; these tentacles have a relatively strong sting for a mushroom anemone. Unfortunately, the large size and capacity to deliver a strong sting can mean trouble for reef keepers with lots of small fishes and crustaceans. *Amplexidiscus* will eat just about anything they can capture. The one shown here is eating a mussel. Photo by MP and C. Piednoir, Aqua Press.

One of the true anemones of the order Actiniaria. Unlike the reef-building corals and many of the other cnidarians, the actiniarians number among themselves many species that are not truly tropical species; some, in fact, come from polar regions. The species shown here, *Anthopleura balli,* is from temperate waters. Photo by MP and C. Piednoir, Aqua Press.

ORDER ACTINIARIA: THE TRUE ANEMONES

The order Actiniaria comprises the true sea anemones, of which there are about 100 species. They are simple in design, having a muscular base or foot that provides a means of attachment to the substrate, a column (body) and a disc that is covered with tentacles. They also have a relatively large centrally located mouth that leads to the gastrovascular cavity.

Like most other cnidarians, anemones reproduce both sexually and asexually. Asexual reproduction is carried out by means of both longitudinal fission and pedal laceration. When anemones reproduce by longitudinal fission they simply split themselves right down the middle, and both halves grow to become two separate individuals. Pedal laceration,

on the other hand, is carried out when an anemone moves over a surface and leaves behind small fleshy pieces of its foot, which can slowly grow into new individuals. Sexual reproduction is carried out by means of spawning when anemones spew forth clouds of eggs and sperm into the water, leading to the formation of free-floating larvae that later settle on the bottom. In

An attractive carpet anemone in the mode with which many anemones are identified: playing host to a guest clownfish.

Closeup of the mouth of a large carpet anemone, *Stichodactyla haddoni*. The particular animal in the photo was big enough and had a sting powerful enough to enable it to kill and eat a large yellow tang (*Acanthurus flavescens*).

some cases anemones will also brood larvae by holding them inside until they are more developed, releasing them later.

While only the shallow-water tropical species of anemones have zooxanthellae, all have the ability to sting using nematocysts, and many can capture prey as small as plankton or as large as fish. In fact, anemones will take all sorts of prepared foods given to them, including bits of meats such as clam or shrimp, and many large anemones will even take live goldfish or minnows. If they are fed such foods they will grow very quickly and reach full size in a short time.

Of the dozens of species, only a few are commonly available to hobbyists. These species are almost exclusively symbiotic anemones that have formed unique relationships with various fishes (clownfishes of the genera *Amphiprion* and *Premnas* primarily) as well as some types of crabs and shrimps. When an anemone forms such a relationship with one or more clownfish, it provides the fish with a protective shelter. This is possible because the clownfish have become immune to the anemone's sting, while any predator that attempts to bother the clownfish is not. In return for this protection the

clownfish will feed an anemone by collecting bits of food and placing them in the anemone's tentacles. This can be observed in aquariums if small pieces of meat are dropped into the water near an anemone that is hosting these fish.

The anemone *Entacmacea quadricolor* (also known as *Actinia quadricolor*) is commonly called the bubble-tip or bulb anemone and is one of the most popular of all the anemones. Large individuals typically reach a diameter of six to eight inches in the aquarium, with numerous tentacles that are up to a few inches long. These can usually easily be identified by the

A large bubble-tip anemone (*Entacmaea quadricolor)* that, because it was not hosting a clownfish at the time the photo was taken, does not exhibit the "bubbles" typically seen on the ends of the tentacles. The bubbles would soon return if an appropriate clownfish were added to the tank.

Bubble-tip anemones will typically move around quite a bit when first placed in an aquarium in an attempt to find a desirable location. They do best under intense light and prefer a moderate to high current; they will actively seek out such conditions. If they find a spot with good lighting and current they will then usually attach firmly to a piece of rock and remain in that location.

Bubble-tip anemones will play host to several types of clownfish that are available to hobbyists. These include most commonly the maroon clownfish (*Premnas biaculeatus*), the tomato clownfish (*Amphiprion frenatus*), the fire clownfish (*Amphiprion ephippium*) and Clark's clownfish (*Amphiprion clarkii*, which is commonly confused with the sebae clownfish, *A. sebae*).

presence of a large bubble-like swelling near the tip of each tentacle, but in some cases the bubbles are absent. This is thought to occur when an anemone has no clownfish symbiont, as it has been observed that the bubbles return if a clownfish takes residence in an anemone that previously had no bubbles.

These anemones may occasionally be found living as solitary individuals but are much more often found living in large groups of hundreds of individuals covering considerable areas of reef. When this is the case, the colony is a result of asexual reproduction by fission, and the individual anemones are relatively small in size. They will many times reproduce in this manner in the aquarium, forming numerous clones.

Actinia equina, very hardy in temperate-water tanks, but generally not suited to truly tropical conditions; this wide-ranging species is very aggressive. Photo by MP and C. Piednoir, Aqua Press.

A long-tentacled anemone, *Macrodactyla doreensis,* called by some a corkscrew anemone.

The anemone *Macrodactyla doreensis* is commonly called the long-tentacle or corkscrew tentacle anemone. This species is very hardy and relatively large, with individuals commonly reaching a diameter of twelve to eighteen inches across the disc. The tentacles are also large, reaching lengths of eight to ten inches. Also, like many other anemones, the long-tentacle anemone can be found in a variety of different colors, and some are striped. They are also usually found living as solitary individuals with their discs lying flat over the substrate and their tentacles corkscrewing up into the water.

Long-tentacle anemones also will typically move around in an attempt to find a desirable location when first placed into an aquarium. And, like the bubble-tip anemone, they prefer intense light and a moderate to high current. However, instead of attaching to a piece of rock, the long-tentacle anemone prefers to attach its base in the bottom of a hole or crevice when in an aquarium. This allows the anemone to expand out of the hole and also allows it a place to withdraw and retreat into if disturbed.

Long-tentacle anemones also will play host to a few different clownfishes. These include the skunk clownfish (*Amphiprion perideraion*) and Clark's clownfish; while it is less common they will occasionally be occupied by the maroon clownfish.

Another popular anemone, *Heteractis malu*, is commonly called the sebae anemone. This anemone typically reaches a diameter of up to one foot in the aquarium, but it has relatively short tentacles, only an inch or two long. In the wild *H. malu* are usually found living as solitary individuals with their discs spread out over the substrate and their bases rooted deep into the sediments of a sandy bottom.

Sebae anemones also will move around when first placed into an aquarium, but unlike many other anemones they prefer an area with a lower current and will not stay in an area in which it is strong. They also prefer to attach their bases in the bottom of a hole or crevice in the same manner as a long-tentacle anemone. Again, this allows the anemone to expand out of the hole while allowing it a place to withdraw and retreat into if disturbed. Unlike many other host anemones, sebae anemones will serve as host for only two species of clownfish. Only Clark's clownfish and the sebae clownfish will inhabit them.

Two similar anemones that belong to the same genus are *Stichodactyla gigantea* and *Stichodactyla haddoni,* the

Stichodactyla haddoni with disk in normal position.

Right: Phlyctenanthus australis, an Australian species; note the bubble-like vesicles covering the animal's column. Photo by U. Erich Friese.

Below: Tealia lofotensis, a non-tropical species, exhibiting the gracefully draped tentacles that have helped to create at least part of the mystique surrounding the "flower animals." Photo by U.Erich Friese.

carpet or saddle anemones. Both of these anemones can grow to very large sizes, commonly reaching a diameter of over two feet. Both have a large disc that can either lie flat over the substrate or can fold up in a shape that resembles a saddle, and the main distinction between the two is their tentacles. The disc of *Stichodactyla gigantea* is completely covered with short tapering tentacles that are only about half an inch to an inch in length. *Stichodactyla haddoni*, on the other hand, has a disc that is densely covered with tiny bubble-like tentacles.

These anemones are always found as solitary individuals firmly attached to hard sub-strates. But like many other anemones, when first placed into an aquarium they will move around quite a bit at times in search of a favorable spot to settle down. They do best under intense light and prefer a moderate current; like many others, they prefer to attach their bases in the bottom of a hole or crevice, giving them a place to retreat to if bothered.

Stichodactyla gigantea will play host to several popular clownfish species, including Clark's clownfish, the skunk clownfish and the percula clownfishes (the look-alikes *A. percula* and *A. ocellaris*) as well as several others. *Stichodactyla haddoni*, on the other hand, will not play host for the percula clownfish or skunk clownfish, but will host instead the saddleback clownfish (*Amphiprion polymnus*) and sebae clownfish, as well as a few others.

The anemone *Heteractis magnifica* (formerly called *Radianthus ritteri*) is commonly called Ritter's anemone or the ritteri or the magnificent anemone. This is a very large anemone, with individuals commonly reaching a diameter of two feet. The numerous tentacles are up to a few inches long and can be almost completely enclosed by the base when the anemone is disturbed.

H. magnifica is most commonly found living as solitary individuals living out in the open attached to large rocks

Stichodactyla helianthus. The *Stichodactyla* species vary in the degree to which they are accepted as hosts by different anemonefish species. Photo by U. Erich Friese.

Right: An individual of a *Condylactis* species. The genus provides some beautiful anemones, but they are not regarded as normal hosts for anemonefishes.

on the reef. They enjoy the strong currents received by living unsheltered and also prefer intense lighting. Unfortunately, often they do not ship very well and arrive at stores dead or very ill. For this reason it is always a good idea to let a ritteri anemone stay at a store under observation for a few days before purchasing one. Another problem hobbyists have with this anemone is

Below: *Heteractis magnifica* doing what comes naturally—serving as a ready host for *Amphiprion*. Photo by U. Erich Frise

its tendency to constantly wander about the aquarium. The species has a very strong sting and can burn the flesh of other corals and anemones, making a roving *H. magnifica* very undesirable.

If ritteri anemones are kept in sparsely populated aquariums or decide to settle into a particular spot and stop wandering they can be wonderful specimens simply because they will accept any clownfish placed in the aquarium. They accept not only the more common clownfishes such as the percula, maroon, tomato, fire, clarkii, sebae and skunk clownfishes but also many others that are less common, such as the saddleback clownfish.

Probably the most popular anemone that is not a host anemone is *Condylactis gigantea*. This anemone is commonly called a condy anemone or Haitian anemone and is one of the most commonly seen anemones in stores. While there are Pacific species of *Condylactis*, most if not all of those for sale are collected in Florida waters or in the Caribbean and are very inexpensive. Many are very colorful, and large

individuals can reach sizes of up to ten inches in the aquarium. But, as mentioned, they do not typically play host to clownfishes. Only on rare occasions do clarkii and sebae clownfish form a relationship with them, usually only if there is no other host anemone in the aquarium.

To end the discussion of anemones, one more common type must be mentioned, the anemones of the genus *Aiptasia*. These are commonly referred to as rock anemones or glass anemones, and while being attractive in appearance they are not host anemones, and they can be a horrible nuisance for the hobbyist. These small anemones reach a size of only one or two inches in height and are easily recog-

nized by their delicate tentacles, which are brown to almost clear in color, and by their appearance on live rock. They are usually introduced into the aquarium unintentionally when new live rock is purchased and can reproduce very quickly, covering a piece of rock and spreading out over more area. While the idea of free anemones that reproduce well sounds great at first, unfortunately they have the potential to severely irritate or even kill almost anything they come into contact with. They have a strong sting and once established in an aquarium are almost impossible to get rid of. To avoid them, carefully inspect live rock, and do not purchase pieces that are "infested."

Aiptasia, the so-called glass anemones that are among the biggest pests that marine aquarists encounter. Added inadvertently to an aquarium, these small anemones can multiply quickly and spread throughout the tank, stinging everything they touch. The one pictured below is burning polyps in its immediate vicinity.